Outfoxed!

A Tale for Leaders, Professionals, and Other Precocious Children

David E. Bricker

Outfoxed!

A Tale for Leaders, Professionals, and Other Precocious Children

By Dave Bricker
All Rights Reserved.
Copyright ©2022 Essential Absurdities Press

Cover and book design by David Bricker.

ISBN: 978-0-9862960-7-9

ESSENTIAL ABSURDITIES PRESS

Outfoxed!

**A Tale for Leaders, Professionals,
and Other Precocious Children**

David E. Bricker

1

A Journey Begins

MOLE EMERGED from his tunnel one fine fall day. He breathed in the foresty forest smells and marveled at the woodlands' orange and brown and yellow glow. Inspired by the crisp morning air he smiled. *I believe I shall enjoy a walk down the path today.*

And because, dear reader, this story is a short one, it was in the very next paragraph that Mole encountered Python.

"Ah, Python my friend. I should have worn my feather *boa*."

"Never heard that one before," grumbled Python. "Didn't you greet me with that line the last six times we…?"

"Force of habit," said Mole, excusing himself. "I'll make a note to work on something new…. How have you been, my friend?"

Back in his day, Python had been adept at stalking with stealth, grabbing his prey, holding them in his coils, and squeezing until all the gooey goodness popped out of them. But word had gotten out and Python was finding it more and more difficult to hunt successfully.

Mole, once he was certain that Python wasn't going to squish, squash, strangle, and devour him, had become his friend and confidant.

"I'm doing just grand," said Python, "and I'm *loving* this weather!"

"So here we are," said Mole, "two talking animals in a woodland setting. Sounds like a cheesy setup for a story. How shall we get on with it?"

Python coiled himself up next to Mole and thought for a moment. "It's the twenty-first century so we'll have to consider a few things before we can get the green light to begin an adventure."

"Ah *that,*" acknowledged Mole. "Storytelling used to be so much simpler. Well … we're two different species. I suppose that covers the diversity angle but we're still two dudes in the woods. How can we tick the gender inclusion box?"

"Well, it's not my call to make," said Python with a note of feigned concern, "but some of the characters in our journey will surely have to be female."

"That's it!" exclaimed Mole. "And it says here in the script that we'll be traveling to meet Fox.

How much do you want to bet that Fox is of the feminine persuasion?"

"I'm sure you're right," said the snake, "so let's get on with this mole and python show before our readers bail."

"Good plan," agreed Mole. "So we've had our chance encounter on a regular, happy, sunny day and we know that our journey will involve going to see Fox but…"

"You're right!" exclaimed Python. "We need a *conflict*—something to drive us—a mission."

"Yes," said Mole, "and it has to be a conflict our readers can identify with—something that makes *our* journey a metaphor for *their* journey."

"Funny how stories work," offered Python. "Tell someone what to do and more often than not, they'll thank you for the advice and continue doing whatever foolish thing got them in trouble in the first place…"

Mole nodded.

"…but tell them a *story* about *someone else* and they're all eyes and ears!" continued Python.

"Yes," said Mole, "especially when the characters are talking animals. Most readers will never suspect that this story is *really about them*."

"And that's one reason stories are transformational," agreed Python, "but we're in *how many* pages and *nothing has happened yet*. There's no threat. There's no opportunity. So far, this is just a big story set-up. I don't know about you but I'm bored."

"We need a conflict," said Python. "What can we do?"

"Let's consult the script," suggested Mole.

"I tried," said Python, "but I have no hands and it's quite difficult to turn the pages. This story isn't exactly ADA-compliant. Do you think you could…?"

"Of course," said Mole. "And I won't complain if you improvise a bit."

"Thank you," said Python.

Mole adjusted his glasses, shuffled through the pages for a moment or two, and then looked quizzically at his companion. "I haven't run into anything like this before. It seems we have some choices."

"Should we call our union rep?" asked Python.

"No. Run with it. If we screw this up we can always blame the writer. Let's just do this gig and get paid."

"Gotcha," said Python. "So you mentioned some choices…."

"Yes," said Mole. "Here are some possibilities:

"One: The conflict in our story can be that it's a gorgeous autumn day in the woods. Everything's easy and we have no reason to complain … but we're not satisfied. The world is bathed in the woodlands' 'orange and brown and yellow glow' and yet ennui has set in. The conflict is that we need a conflict."

"Clever metaphor, that," observed Python.

"The autumn day? Yes, I caught that, too," replied Mole.

Python adjusted his coils. "I suppose that *is* a problem for a lot of people. No growth. No challenges. They're just going through the motions and they're bored. Some readers are sure to identify with that one … but let's dive deeper."

"There is another route:" offered Mole. "The folks in casting did their homework. You're here because you *used to* be an effective hunter. You *used to* hunt your prey and *squeeze* them but the old techniques aren't working anymore. Do you think that could be a metaphor for sales?"

"Maybe," said Python. "But times and technology have changed. The language and culture have evolved. We had to sort out all that diversity stuff before we could even get started, right? We never had to do that in the old days. And though some people sell products and services, other people sell ideas—leadership, philosophies, perspectives. 'Selling' can work but only if we acknowledge that the definition of selling has changed."

"That's good," said Mole. "Did you improvise that?"

"I've been pondering this for a while so yes and no. We're all selling all the time, don't you think?

Maybe you're asking for a raise or a date or trying to convince your boss that *your* idea is the one to run with. It's *all* selling."

"You're onto something," said Mole. "So in this scenario, the *conflict* is that you're the 'old snake' who has found that 'putting the squeeze' on customers and treating them like 'prey' isn't producing the results it used to."

"I suppose," sighed Python. "But I am going to enjoy a rat or two when this gig is over."

"*Shh!* Your mic is hot … and I certainly won't be joining you for dinner," scolded Mole, "But why do you think *I'm* here? I mean … I'm grateful for the gig but why does this story need a mole in it?"

"I suppose we have to nail that down before we can begin our quest. Otherwise, you'll just be along for the ride," said Python.

"And being a sidekick is just dull," said Mole.

"So what's *my* conflict? What makes *me* go see Fox?"

"Hmm," hissed Python. "If we don't get this show on the road, this production will be an epic snooze-fest—and it'll be the same for our readers; they're looking for a new adventure; that's why they're here. So there's me with my outdated persuasion and influence techniques that no longer work in a rapidly-changing world."

"Readers will identify with that problem," said Mole, "but why am *I* here? Maybe they couldn't afford Ryan Reynolds?"

Python flicked his tongue and gave Mole a sidelong glance. "I have an idea: Explain to me how you dig your tunnels."

Mole closed his eyes, twisted his chin, and reflected on Python's question. "I can't say exactly," he confessed. "I don't know. I just *dig*. It's what I've always done. I could tell you how I use my paws to move the dirt but that wouldn't really be *it*. I just…"

"And that's your conflict," suggested Python. "You have a talent but you can't codify it. You can't quantify it. You can't explain it. And that means you can't teach it to others and you can't scale it."

"I guess that's why I've always had such a difficult time selling it," confessed Mole. "People ask what I do and…"

"And that's why we're both working as part-time storybook characters," said Python with a chuckle. "So what you *do* is dig tunnels … but what you have to *offer* is something much more valuable. And if you can't articulate what that value is…"

"Excellent" said the Mole. "I'm sorry I've never worked with you before. I think we have a story now!"

"Yes," said Python, "But allow me to reinforce our plot before we go. During my life as a cold-blooded predator, I heard thousands of animals appeal to me to spare their lives. Most of them talked about *themselves:* They'd tell me what *they* were really good at or about the families *they* had to support … and I'd apologize to them, explain that some of us woodland folk just weren't designed to subsist on nuts and berries and grubs, and then well … you know … down the hatch. Nothing personal; it's just business."

"Hey! That's another great metaphor!" exclaimed Mole. "Probably some of our readers are battling business challenges! What if this whole surviving in the woods theme is just…?"

"Yes," said Python. "Precisely! Maybe there's hope for our writer after all … but to continue my story, every once in a while I'd find myself coiled around someone who knew how to frame their important message—**PLEASE DON'T EAT ME!**—in a way that made me let them go. Instead of whining about themselves, they convinced me they had *something to offer*. True—most of my prospects ended up as lunch meat—Spam—but of the few who knew how to communicate their value, some even became my friends."

"So I think what you're saying, Python, is that my reason for going on our Fox quest is that though I'm a good digger, I don't know how to … how did you say it … 'communicate my value?'"

"*Every* mole is a good digger," explained Python, "but that's cost-of-entry. You make tunnels and ruin the golf course like every other mole." Python yawned. "But what differentiates you from all those other moles? Are you 'junk mail' or someone people want to read about?"

Mole's eyes moistened. "I don't know."

"And now we have our conflicts," proclaimed Python. "Collectively, we have to discover our authentic value so we can *not* get eaten … and because we have to eat, we have to find new ways to hunt. Prospects have gotten smarter."

"Now we've got some fur and scales in this game!" said Mole, his face brightening. "This is all about survival isn't it?"

"Yes, but we have one more problem," said Python. "We need a trigger event—something that sets us off on our journey to see Fox. What could inspire us to undertake a long, difficult adventure on a delightful autumn day?"

Mole took a deep breath. "We could go the traditional route where you and I start griping about our boredom and our respective personal and professional struggles until one of us suggests we should go ask Wise Old Owl. Then we'll hike on over to the oh-so-cliché hollow tree where Owl will ask us a few mystical-sounding questions, tell us we need to go see Fox, and charge us an exorbitant consulting fee that probably isn't covered in our contracts."

"How about we skip that and just enjoy a few cold ones in my trailer?" suggested Python.

"Excellent idea," agreed Mole. "Owl gives me the creeps, anyway. Let's pick up the story in chapter 2."

Send Me a Sign

PYTHON AND MOLE scrambled up and down hills and ravines, forded streams, and hiked over rocky terrain and verdant woodlands. The path climbed ever higher as they approached the top of Mount Metaphor where Fox lived. The sun arced slowly across the sky to mark the passage of time with a simple literary device.

"What a schlep!" complained Mole. "You make this look easy, Python. What's your secret?"

"I'm extremely flexible ... and I couldn't ask for a lower center of gravity," explained Python.

"I suppose that's Nature's compensation for not giving me any limbs."

Mole stopped and stood with his paws on his knees, catching his breath. "I wasn't expecting all this marathon mountain-climbing business. My agent's gonna hear about this!"

"If Fox was easy to get to, our story wouldn't be interesting," said Python. "Good story-telling involves some sort of quest—an odyssey—a journey. The writer has us climbing up a mountain to find the teacher. It's classic story stuff … and it's analogous to the work our readers will have to do to achieve their own transformation."

"Hey! I'll bet something surprising will happen at any moment," observed Mole.

"I was thinking the same thing: That's how stories work," replied Python. "But I guess we're too smart for this. Whatever it is won't be a very surprising surprise."

"Maybe it's time for the scene where the 'relentless' sun appears with a big lens flare!" said Mole.

"Yes," agreed Python, "And they always add the sound of a hawk—as if that's somehow relevant to *anything!*"

"Oy!" cried Mole. "You have no idea how many times I've heard that and dived into my burrow!"

Python nodded. "Me, too…. So Mole, skip a page or two and jump to the scene where we just can't stand the idea of taking *one more step* … even if I don't actually take steps because I'm a snake. My belly's getting sore."

"What's with the pacing here?" cried Mole in desperation. "I need some plotline to work with!

Please! Somebody! Give me a sign!"

"Here! I think I found one," said Python.

And as if it had been planted there that same day by the set team, a colorful wooden sign revealed itself among the weeds by the side of the path:

"I suppose I *am* getting tired," said Mole.

Python shook his head and the two continued up the path.

Before long, the pair encountered a second sign, this one planted right in the middle of the trail.

"Someone's got that right," said Mole. "I'm bushed!"

Python sighed. "Almost there!"

"What do you mean?" asked his companion.

"Rule of threes," explained the snake. "In storytelling you get three wishes … or you have to find the three magic gems or … if someone's making a speech they tend to group things in threes—like "blood, sweat, and tears."

"Interesting," replied Mole. "Churchill actually said 'blood, toil, tears, and sweat.'"

Python chuckled. "Yes, and people could only remember three of those words, and they remembered them in the wrong order. Three is the key!"

"Sounds like the writer is trying to wedge in some sort of lesson here," complained Mole. "It's a real story-stopper."

"A talking mole and a talking python exchanging observations about Winston Churchill while they hike up a mountain to meet a fox does strike me as a bit contrived but I'll bet that third sign's going to pop up soon," said Python.

"Cue the orchestra! Here it is!" cried Mole. "Couldn't have happened fast enough."

Python took a deep breath.

"I'm gasterflabbed," said Mole. "What do you think these signs mean?"

"They mean," replied Python, "that we've hit the end of another chapter. We've come to the end of this step on our journey and we've been presented with a conundrum—with a puzzle to solve. We'll surely be left hanging until the next chapter … and so will the reader."

"Why do writers do that?" asked Mole.

Python drew a small instructional circle in the air with the tip of his tail. "It's a minor cliff-hanger that gives the story a place to rest … and at the same time, it compels the reader to come back and turn the page. The writer's designing in a place where the network can cut to a commercial or the reader can put the story down, process their regret over having started to read it in the first place, and then pick it up later. It's their way of 'controlling the dosage.' Just watch. It'll happen every chapter."

Mole sat down on a rock and looked at his friend. "So before we make the obligatory observation that the sun is getting low and acknowledge that it's been a long day of climbing and decide to set up our camp under that oh-so-convenient rock outcropping over there, I find myself wondering…"

"Yes!" interrupted Python. "Is this whole journey just some sort of bizarre treatise on storytelling?"

"Could be," agreed Mole, "but since that gives us a *second* cliffhanger to end this chapter with, let's just cut to the scene where it's gotten dark and we're saying 'good night' to each other just before we nod off."

"Good idea," said Python. "And since we got that scene in the can last week, they can add it in post-production."

"So off to the pub then?" asked Mole.

"Sorry but no," grumbled Python. "I'd love to but I've got a gig with a plumber tonight."

"Ah well … see ya tomorrow then."

3

The Big Pitch

PYTHON AND MOLE rose with the morning sun and continued their journey. No sooner had they resumed their climb up the rocky path, they found themselves confronted by a shabby, furry figure who flashed them a toothy grin.

Jackal extended a welcoming paw. "Good morning, gentleman; good morning—and a very *good* good morning it is, wouldn't you agree? I'm afraid you have me at a disadvantage as I'm wholly unprepared … but I'm always true to my word or my name's not Marvin."

Python and Mole looked at one another mutely as the writer hadn't given them any lines.

Jackal continued his rapidfire soliloquy. "Pardon my lack of discretion but I couldn't help but notice that *this* path—*the very one* we happen to be standing on together this fine morning—only runs in *two* directions—upward and downward. And since you two travelers appear to be of the upward-climbing variety—you will find yourselves *most grateful* to be informed of the *absolute latest* developments in alpine apparatii for the discriminating adventurer."

Mole thumbed through his script and whispered back at Python. "It's all him. We've got nothing!"

Python rolled his eyes.

Jackal resumed his greeting. "But excuse me friends, I've gotten ahead of myself. How rude of me! How rude! *I* am Jackal—slayer of damsels, rescuer of dragons, barker of carnivals, earl of sandwich, oil of olay, table of offsets, tincture of iodine, and experienced professional expert offering professional expertise in all things relevant, relatable, debatable, deflatable, conflatable, and commercially expedient. Gentlemen, how may I place myself in your service?"

"I thought your name was Marvin," said Python.

Jackal looked uncomfortable and then composed himself. "But of course! My *good* friends— my *best* friends—call me Marvin, and because I have a feeling we're all going to be the best of pals, you may consider yourselves free to refer to me by my more familiar appellation."

"'Alpine' and 'appellations?'" mused Python. "Our writer loves a rocky pun."

"Yes," said Mole. "But let's stay in character, shall we?"

Python nodded. "Sorry."

"Thank you for that wonderful introduction!" said Mole to Jackal. "I am Mole and this is Python, my friend and traveling companion. We're …"

"On your way to visit Fox?" interrupted Jackal.

"Yes! Yes! How did you know?" asked Mole.

"My finely-honed powers of deduction are acute, moot, and astute," explained Jackal. "And given that there's *nothing* but no one and no one but *nothing* at the end of this trail other than Fox and *very little* to be found betwixt and be-tween … *and* … given that this is *only chapter 3* of a *slow-moving* story that takes place on this very slope of a quite-metaphorical mountain, my fine mind has discerned that you two customers … er … travelers … could only be engaged on a mighty quest. You seek *transformation!*"

Mole smiled. "Well, we certainly…"

"You certainly do indeed!" interjected Jackal. "And that's why you'll be profoundly, deeply, and quite-stupendously glad to discover that I took it upon myself to check my inventory this very morning and verify with only the very sleightest degree of inaccuracy that I have *two* left in stock— *only two*—but how *fortuitous* for you because if I'm right—and I most often am—it appears to be the case that there are *two of you*—an alignment of happenstance, coincidence, kismet, improbable concurrence, and not-so-clever writing of *celestial proportions!*"

"Thank you," said Python, "but we have a long day of climbing ahead and…"

"Of course you do! Of course you do!" barked Jackal. "And I've been remiss in not presenting my offer with greater immediacy, expediency, and specificity!"

"There's that rule of threes again," hissed Python to Mole.

And with that, Jackal reached behind a conveniently-located rock and produced his merchandise: two rather ordinary-looking branches. "Allow me to introduce the most princely of prizes for the serious, imperious, and delirious traveler—the Stick-2-It® Hiker's Helper. Why *struggle* up the path of life when you need only lean on this quality bough of oak, precision-engineered by nature herself and hewn only yesterday from the mighty trunk from which it was so recently affixed? Lesser purveyors who trade in inferior equipment might offer a selection of wood species, customized lengths, and fine finishes but here at Stick-2-It, we have you the customer in mind—yes! Why subject yourselves to an incommodious selection process? Why *think* when the time is nigh to *act?* Why…?"

"It's a branch!" complained Python, his annoyance beginning to show.

"I can see how you might think such a thought," said Jackal, "but please don't be fooled by such foolishness! Stick-2-It is no mere branch—no common stalk—not some mundanity to be dismissed as a simple sprig! It's never-ending, highly-trending, patent-pending and endowed with numerous other compound adjectives carefully crafted by linguists to facilitate the expression of adoration for which I shall soon have to procure more hyphens. No, my friends; this is no *branch*— and these two specimens I make available to you today are my *last two* — the ultimate and penultimate pieces remaining in this terrestrial realm! And once they're gone … well … Would you continue up the steep and rocky inclinations and declinations of this story's tyrannical terrain unprepared? Ill-equipped? *Ipso facto carpe diem soup du jour?*"

"How much?" asked Mole.

"Ah, my boy, you needn't concern yourself with *trifling* matters. Price is no object. When presented with that rare coalescence of *high quality* and *limited supply,* questions of cost become mere distractions from our mutual pursuit of *value* — that quest for which *binds us together* as *dear friends and companions.* Let us aspire to guide our discourse to follow loftier designs, grander purposes, and…"

"It's a branch!" asserted Python. "Thank you very much for your time, Jackal. Mole, let's hit the trail!"

"Ah but my friends, you misjudge, begrudge, and besmudge! And you force from me a most uncomfortable confession: Though my appearance may belie my true condition, I've fallen on difficult times. Your kind patronage will help me recover from maladies far too numerous, serious, and extemporaneously contrived to mention; resurrect my recently-departed grandmother; and forestall foreclosure on the home that has been my family's only refuge for generations."

"I'm so sorry," said Mole. "How can we...?"

"There's always a family home and an evil banker waiting to call in the debt," noted Python with a hiss.

"You can't beat the classics," said Jackal. "Nevertheless, having been afflicted by great suffering I beseech you kind sirs to…"

"Nonsense," declared Python flatly.

"But Python," cried Mole. "The trail is steep. We could use some clever climbing contraptions … and we can't just leave poor Marvin with…"

"Actually, we can and we will!" said Python. And with that, he rolled Mole up in his coils and whisked him up the trail.

4

Tough Customers

WHAT WAS THAT!?" asked Mole with tremulant incredulity?

"Stop it!" admonished Python.

"Stop what?" inquired Mole.

"Not you, Mole. The writer's stuck in some sort of quasi-Victorian idiom. *'Tremulant incredulity?' Really?* Now that we're out of that idiot Jackal's sight, can we *please* go back to standard English, Mr. Dickens?"

"I'll start over," suggested Mole. "Take 2."

"Thank you," said Python.

"What was that!?" asked Mole with great surprise.

"Much better. Thank you," said Python. "You were about to buy a common tree branch from a guy who looked the product of a sexual union between a mangy hyena and an overstuffed vacuum cleaner bag!"

"But I thought Marvin…"

"His name isn't Marvin," said Python, "and I know a predator when I see one!"

"You really think…?"

"Yes, Mole. *I really think,*" said Python. "You came *this close* to getting scammed … but I *am* starting to see the purpose of your character in this story."

"Well thank you for saving me from certain bamboozlement," replied Mole. "What are your thoughts about my character's purpose?"

Python took a deep breath. "As we travel up this mountain and encounter the various teachers and challenges that are essential to good storytelling, I believe you will discover the strength and insight to become a smart consumer, and in that…"

"Oh no!" cried Mole. "I accidentally tore the tag off a pillow once. I ended up hiding from the Consumer for three weeks! I could have been *consumed*—eaten!"

"No, no—not *that* kind of consumer," assured Python. "We are *all* consumers of food, media, goods and services, and stories of questionable quality. Some of us are more easily manipulated by lies and distortions than others. Back when I was a young lad in snake school, we were taught a number of effective hunting techniques: a comforting smile, smooth talk, an irresistible offer of something in short supply. Before long my dinner prospects and I would be best buddies. I'd have my tail resting affectionately on their shoulder and then … well … you know what happened next!"

"How come you never consumed *me?*" asked Mole timidly.

"You needn't worry," said Python. "Moles taste like tilapia—like mud!"

"How do you know?" inquired Mole.

"Never mind that," Python replied, "but when the copyright expired on the Snake Manual and it fell into the public domain, all the forest folk read it. They can spot a predator in an instant."

"Wow! How do you eat?" asked Mole.

"All my meals are processed or frozen these days," confessed Python, "but I'm a Python and

I'm still a hunter at heart. That doesn't mean I can't be friends with animals I might normally eat—I'm not heartless—but it does mean I'd like to discover some new techniques. I feel powerless. Whether or not I ever squeeze and squish my prey again isn't the issue—you'd be amazed at what they can do with texturized vegetable protein and tofu these days—but how do you appeal to an *educated* prospect? How do you build confidence and grow relationships with skeptics when your survival depends on it? How do you sell smart ideas to smart people?"

"So back in Chapter 3…?"

"Yep. Jackal threw all sorts of flowery language at you. The signs we encountered in Chapter 2 were designed to soften us up. He offered us a pair of *absolutely unremarkable* branches he'd clipped off a random tree moments before he met us, and claimed they were the last two available. And then, when I didn't fall for his scheme, he made his big mistake."

"What's that?" asked Mole.

"He played the victim card."

"The victim card?"

"Never play the victim card—on stage or in life," declared Python. "At the beginning of Jackal's sales pitch, he talked about how his hiking sticks would help us on our climb. He talked about his product in terms of its benefits; that's the only thing he did right."

"Okay ... but what about the victim card?" asked Mole.

"When Jackal saw I wasn't falling for his bogus pitch, he appealed to our better nature. He tried to make *his* imaginary problems *our* imaginary problems."

"And I felt bad for him," said Mole. "I was reaching for my wallet when you…"

"Yes," said Python, "but when Jackal first approached us, he was happy and enthusiastic and helpful—if perhaps a bit full of himself. It wasn't until he was about to lose his meal ticket that he became desperate and hungry and hopeless."

"In other words," replied Mole. "It wasn't until his scheme failed that he flip-flopped and began to beg."

"And when was the last time you saw begging do anything positive for a relationship?" asked Python. "Had he approached *without* making a phony offer and just asked us for a few coins, I would have been tempted."

"I'm embarrassed," said Mole. "I shouldn't have fallen for that malarkey. I should have seen through Jackal's..."

"I'm sure you will next time," said Python.

"What about you?" asked Mole.

"My victory at this point is that I think you understand me better," said Python. "The woods are full of tacky operators selling flimsy products and useless services and third-rate ideas. Caught in a feeding frenzy, they scheme and connive and lie and exaggerate in a swirling cloud of circular imitation. Each thinks the others know how the game should be played and in their eagerness to win, they don't even notice that the smart consumers—the *really juicy* ones—are walking away!"

"Sorry to change the subject, Python, but I wonder," said Mole. "How far have we traveled in this chapter?"

"In real time, probably a few hundred yards," speculated Python, "but in story time we probably have enough discussion down to call this chapter a wrap."

"But nothing much happened," protested Mole.

"I'm sure they can edit in some hiking scenes and make it look like we've covered some miles. I don't think you'll object to not having to actually climb very far today."

"I'm okay with that," said Mole with a chuckle. "I'm still sore from yesterday."

Python nodded his approval. "And you did learn some important lessons about marketing and self-awareness. Character development counts as 'something happening,' doesn't it?"

"I suppose," said Mole. "So all we need now is some signal to our readers that we'll find a new challenge to deal with in chapter 5."

"Is there one in the script?"

"Oh yes. Here it is," said Mole. "Mysterious footprints."

"I can work with that," said Python, "and look— here they are!"

Mole stood with his forepaws on his hips and stared at the ground before them. "Should we puzzle and ponder for a few moments and wonder what we're about to get into?"

"Nah, all the fear and hesitation we need is implied," said Python. "They'll add a big diminished chord to the soundtrack and dial up the tension. Let's get over to the food tent before the production crew scarfs up all the good stuff."

5

The Tower of Babble

MOLE AND PYTHON continued their trek, climbing and talking as they hiked along the mountain path. By and by, the road led toward the shore of a great lake.

"What's so great about it?" asked Python.

—Python, this is the second chapter in a row where you've disrupted my intro. "You don't have to love the script; you just have to read it! Could you possibly just...?

"Did you hear that?" asked Python.

"This lake *is* great!" exclaimed Mole, coming to the aid of his friend and further delaying the continuation of the story.

"I agree," said Python. "I can see the peak of Mount Metaphor off in the distance. And though it appears to be quite a *distant* distance, we should find Fox's home up on that slope *wayyyyy* over there."

"Which also happens to be conveniently located on the far side of this large—and quite great by the way—lake," said Mole.

"So what happened to the footprints from the end of chapter 4?" asked Python.

"Oh here they are!" exclaimed Mole. "Good catch Python. I hope the writer appreciates you plugging that plot hole."

The pair followed the footprints to the shore where a sailing vessel lay tied to a dock.

"That's it?" asked Python. "The oh-so mysterious footprints just lead us to the dock? That's not very exciting."

> —Perhaps, but those prints did provide a bridge to chapter 5. We all got to the lake, right? Could you perhaps get on with the story?

"There's that voice again!" said Mole.

The pair proceeded down the dock where they knocked on the hull of the tidy and well-kept sailing schooner.

The main hatch slid open and a gray figure emerged from the companionway. "Good afternoon to you," said a soft voice. "Captain Wolf at your service, and this is the sailing vessel

Clementine. Are you seeking passage to the far side of the lake?"

"That seems a rather obvious question," whispered Python to Mole, "but at least we've finally got our first female character — *and* a way to get past our next obstacle."

"Yes!" said Mole, ignoring Python's observation. "I am Mole and this is my friend Python. We seek Fox who lives on that mountain *wayyyyy* over there."

"Well I can ferry you across," said Wolf, "but I'm shorthanded today. My crew's got the flumps. You'll have to help with the sailing and navigating."

"We're happy to assist as much as we can," offered Python, "but we're talking forest animals; we don't have much experience with boats."

"It's the same for me but that's what the script calls for," said Captain Wolf.

"Got it," said Python.

"Welcome aboard, then. Let's get going, shall we?" Wolf sat back on a canvas sail bag and gestured for her two passengers to do the same. Crossing her paws, she took a deep breath and spoke seriously. "We *may* face a few challenges along the way. We'll have to navigate past a rocky and shallow shoal … and the weather out on the lake can be precarious this time of year. It's not unusual for a storm to blow up out of nowhere; things can get pretty rough. Are you sure you want to make this trip?"

"I think we're contractually obligated," said Mole.

"So you'll teach us how to operate the boat before we head out?" asked Python.

"Of course," said Captain Wolf. "Sailing is easy!"

Mole and Python made themselves comfortable on their sail bag seats.

Captain Wolf rose to face them, stood behind the mainmast, and began her presentation. "The halyards all have piston shackles spliced to their ends that fasten them to the heads of the sails. Once we've bent the jib to the forestay—it has hanks on its luff for that purpose—we'll fasten the two jib sheets to the clew with simple bowlines and run them aft through the turning blocks to the self-tailing winches. Remember to tie a figure-of-eight knot in the bitter end of each of those lines, please. Looks like the wind's blowing ten-to-fifteen knots from abeam so we'll be able to haul the canvas aloft before we cast the lines off the bollards. Then we'll reach right off the dock! I'll mind the helm so all you'll need to do is trim the sheets. Like I said: *Easy!*"

Maybe this isn't such a good idea," said Python.

"I'm having doubts, too," said Mole.

Captain Wolf looked hurt. "I'm sure you'll pick it up as we go. Once you see how everything works, you'll…"

"We all want to get paid," noted Mole. "Let's go for it. Hopefully the special effects crew will take care of anything particularly unpleasant."

"What about navigating?" asked Python.

Captain Wolf's expression brightened. "We'll head round that point over there to the south." Wolf extended a paw toward the coast. "There's a shallow shelf there so we'll need to stand off at least a mile-and-a-half. Once we pass the marker, we'll turn to starboard and tack upwind to reach our destination. I'll use my parallel rules and the compass rose on the chart to plot our course … and of course, I'll do my best to factor in side-drift and current. Along the way, we'll use the hand-bearing compass to sight lines of position off of various lighthouses and landmarks. That will help us keep to our course. By my estimate, we should make port tomorrow night."

"Now I know why sailors talk about '*dead* reckoning,'" whispered Mole to Python. "I've never felt so lost!"

"And what kind of an idiot casts a *snake* in a sailing scene?" complained Python. "What's next—a stride piano duel? What happened to the good old days when I got to play Kaa in *The Jungle Book* …

and I miss those nature documentaries. Where's Marlin Perkins when you need him?"

"Are we going or not?" asked Captain Wolf. "The director's giving us the stink-eye."

"Give me a moment to confer with my friend," said Mole.

Captain Wolf nodded and the two travelers returned to the dock.

Mole looked at Python. "Are we going sailing?"

"Yes," said Python, "but this chapter's nearly over. The voyage will have to start in chapter 6."

"So how do we wrap this one up?" asked Mole.

Python cleared his throat. "Well this *is* a book about storytelling disguised as a tale for children. What did you think about Wolf's instructions?"

"I felt bad for her," confided Mole. "She obviously knows a great deal about sailing and navigating, but when she tries to explain it…"

"Technobabble!" said Python. "Nothing but incomprehensible jargon."

"Do you think another sailor would have understood her?" asked Mole.

"Sure," replied Python, "but another sailor wouldn't need to hear what she had to say; they would already know the material."

Mole sighed. "And I guess that's why we're standing on the dock making a final decision about whether we want to sail with Captain Wolf."

"Precisely," agreed Python. "I wonder how many lucrative deals get *sunk* — pardon the pun — every day because someone's trying to sell an idea or a product or a relationship in a language that the decision-makers can't understand?"

"I'm sure everything sounds plain and simple to the people selling … but I'm just a talking mole," said Mole.

"Yes. That's the point," Python concurred. "So it's decided. Though the odds are against us ever setting foot on land again, we'll get back on board the *Clementine* and voyage forth in pursuit of our mission."

"Do you think we'll hit any storms?" asked Mole.

"It's a story book!" said Python. "What do *you* think?"

"Great hook to end a chapter on!" said Mole. "Good work!"

6

Rocks and Shoals

THE SCHOONER *CLEMENTINE* left a foamy white wake on the dark waters of the lake as she made her way toward the far shore where *wayyyyy* distant Mount Metaphor rose before them from the horizon to the clouds. The sun retired in an explosion of orange and purple before yielding the heavens to a brilliant moon that painted the surface of the water in shimmering silver and black.

"Now *that's* some scene setting," said Python. "Did you catch how he used '*wayyyyy*' in italics with five Ys in it again?"

"Yes, said Wolf. That's a 'callback.' The writer used it twice in Chapter 5; it adds a note of surprise continuity here."

"Let's get back to the scene," suggested Mole. "I don't think our critiques are appreciated."

Python nodded.

Captain Wolf stood behind the wheel minding the compass, and Mole soon learned to adjust the sheet lines whenever she asked him to "harden up the main a bit" or "crank in the jib a few turns." Python familiarized himself with the nautical chart and discovered to his surprise that just as Wolf had said, it wasn't difficult to plot their course using the parallel rules and chart dividers he found in the ship's navigation table.

"You mean I just *magically* figure that out?" asked Python.

"YouTube," suggested Mole. "I've got a four-bar signal out here."

Python smiled. "Way to save the plot again, Mole!"

"Keep your eyes open for the marker," advised Wolf. "We need to leave it to starboard … er pass to the left of it … or we'll risk running up on the rocks."

"Well by my reckoning, we're way too close to shore," said Python. "We're going to miss that mark by a quarter-mile!"

"At least we know where the expression 'missing the mark' came from," suggested Mole.

"So many common phrases have nautical origins," said Captain Wolf. "The one about 'the bitter end' has nothing to do with the bitterness of failure; the 'bitter end' of a rope is the one that gets fastened to the 'bitts' or cleats on the dock. And if you've ever met someone unpredictable who has a bad temper, imagine being on an old warship on a rough and rolling sea when a 'loose cannon' started careening around the deck."

"Each one of those phrases is a story encapsulated into a few words," observed Mole.

Wolf continued. "And though today we say a vessel is 'under way'—as in 'making her way through the water,' the original usage was 'under weigh'—which implied that the ship had 'weighed anchor' and was no longer connected to the sea bottom. In fact, 'weighing anchor' has its own…"

"I'm afraid your little etymology lesson has altogether missed the point," said Python. "We're headed for the rocks!"

"The compass says we're headed due west," said Captain Wolf.

"And what evidence do you have that the compass is accurate?" inquired Python. "Is this your boat?"

"No," confessed Captain Wolf. "I think they rented it for the production, but…"

"Well if we're headed due west, how come the sun set *over there?*" Python jabbed his tail off to the right.

"That's very clever," said Mole. "What made you pay attention to *that?*"

"I'm just reading the script," replied Python, "but if it's all the same to you, let's adjust our course. Worst case is I'm wrong and we lose a few miles by passing too far to the left of the marker. At least we'll still be in the deep water."

Captain Wolf shrugged. "Can you loosen up the sheetlines, Mr. Mole? I'll fall off."

"Don't fall off; we need you!" cried Mole.

Wolf smiled. "No, no. I'll fall off the wind, not off the boat!" And with that, she turned the wheel and *Clementine* began to veer to port.

The trio enjoyed the fresh breeze and the whooshing of the waves in silence as the bow of their vessel plowed a furrow across the lake. Python plotted occasional fixes on the chart as the moon washed all but the brightest stars from the sky.

"I think I see something ahead!" cried Mole.

"It's the marker," said Python with confidence. "I'll bet my Buick on it!"

"You have a Buick?" asked Captain Wolf. "What year?"

"No … just a taste for alliteration," replied Python, "but if we continue on this course, we should pass about a hundred feet off the safe side of the marker."

"So who gets the Buick?" asked Mole.

"Never mind," replied Python. "It was just a figure of speech. I'm sorry I mentioned it."

A few minutes later, the crew of the schooner *Clementine* passed the marker just as Python had predicted.

After some time, Mole spoke. "I'm thinking about the whole 'trust your compass' metaphor. That's what you were doing, Captain Wolf— trusting your compass—which is what everyone tells you you're supposed to do. Then Python started plotting our position and *that's* what kept us from sailing up on the rocks."

"Don't look at me," said Captain Wolf. "I'm just reading the script. I don't know jack about sailing."

"Neither do I," said Python, "but Wolf said it well. "'Trusting your compass' may be what everyone tells you you're *supposed* to do … but if you're doing what everyone tells you you're *supposed* to do, you're *not* trusting *your* compass. When I decided to go to sea on a vessel crewed by talking animals who don't know how to sail a toy boat in a bathtub, I chose to trust *my* compass, not the one mounted on the boat."

"What made you think we were off course?" asked Captain Wolf sheepishly.

"Did he *really* just write that?" asked Python.

"Let's move on," suggested Mole.

"So what made me think we were off course…?

Just a feeling … intuition … something seemed off," mused Python.

"That's it!" said Mole. "That feeling was your 'compass.' You honored your inner compass even when the mechanical compass told you you shouldn't!"

"And that's a good lesson to wind up a chapter with," suggested Python. "Let's set up chapter 7 and close up shop for the night. What have we got?"

"I'll recap," said Mole. "We learned a bunch of useless trivia about storytelling devices—phrases with nautical origins and 'callbacks' and alliteration—and we presented an object lesson about what it means to "trust your compass.'"

"That's a good universal conflict," said Captain Wolf. "Sooner or later, *everyone* is faced with a situation where they have to make a choice between what others think is right and what they *believe* is right. Readers will relate to that."

"I hope so," said Python.

Mole continued. "And the chapter was driven by the conflict that we were headed toward the rocks at sea in the middle of the night with — sorry Captain Wolf — no real guidance."

"No offense taken," said Wolf. "One more chapter and this gig is over for me. Next week I'll be working with some strange little pigs who build single-family homes! I just go where the job takes me."

Mole cleared his throat. "And we continued our Journey — our mission to find Fox so she can help me explain my value and help Python learn some new hunting strategies."

"There's another lesson here," suggested Python. "We started off on a sunny autumn day, started discussing our shortcomings and ended up on a quest. Since then we've had to escape from a cheeseball sales pitch, decipher a heap of technobabble, and learn to trust ourselves when our guides weren't up to the task. Every chapter has had its own conflict and its own resolution, and every chapter has set up the conflict for the one that follows it."

"What does that mean?" asked Mole.

"It means," continued Python, "that there's a method to this storytelling madness—a story structure that will keep readers on the rails even when they can't possibly be enjoying the train ride. In this particular narrative, most of the 'rocks and shoals' have been common storytelling mistakes—like hard-sell sales tactics and jargony explanations. If we talking animals can do our jobs as effective metaphorical constructs, our readers just might end up using the power of storytelling to improve their communication skills."

"That's awfully convoluted," said Mole.

"I think I'm finally getting the hang of steering this thing!" said Captain Wolf.

"Good news, that," said Python

"Hey!" cried Mole. "I've got my phone. We could have used the GPS!"

"I thought of that," said Python, "but that's just another way to *not* trust your compass."

"I suppose," said Mole. "And you plugged another plot hole!"

"Oh, did you see that flash?" asked Captain Wolf.

"Wait for it," said Python. "One-thousand-one, one-thousand-two, one-thousand-three, one-thousand…."

A rumble of distant thunder heralded the approach of chapter 7.

7

Overpowered

THE SCHOONER *CLEMENTINE* continued under weigh (Did you catch that?) toward
the far shore. Between the three travelers and
safe harbor boiled an intimidating sky of dark
clouds and lightning. Behind them, the rocky
shoal they'd rounded in chapter 6 threatened to
destroy them if the wind blew them down on it.

"The studio's gonna be pretty upset if we lose
this ship," complained Captain Wolf. "They
won't get their deposit back!"

By and by, the temperature dropped, the wind fell light, and a fog descended over the dull black surface of the lake.

"Start the motor!" called Mole.

"Can't do it," said Python. "This is a storybook. Sailboats don't have motors in storybooks, and if there's a storm on the horizon…"

"There's nothing to do but face the challenge," said Captain Wolf. "And even if we did reveal to readers that this vessel has a perfectly-functioning Perkins 4-108 diesel sitting in the engine box under the companionway ladder, we'd never find the navigation beacon again in this fog. There's nothing we can do but drift until the wind returns."

"I think I understood the important parts of that," said Mole.

"Didn't we get past the technobabble in chapter 5?" asked Python.

"Sorry, boys. Those are my lines," said Captain Wolf. "A character's got to stay consistent … and Mole, don't even think about mentioning GPS."

Another bright flash preceded a loud crack of thunder. A few fat raindrops spattered on the deck.

"Here she comes!" cried Captain Wolf.

"Python, I'm scared!" cried Mole.

"Don't worry, Mole," Python assured him. "You and I are the two main characters—the protagonists. The writer won't kill us off before we finish our journey. That would screw up the whole story."

"You're right!" said Mole. "But what about Captain Wolf?"

"I don't know," said Python. "I guess we all have to keep each other safe. So much for riding this out down below in the cabin!"

The light drumbeat of raindrops on the deck grew to a crescendo. Sheets of rain pelted the *Clementine* and her crew.

"I'm glad I've got scales instead of fur," called Python over the din.

"Nice!" called Mole.

"Yeah … thanks for the empathy there, Python. I'm touched!" cried Wolf.

"Did he really just write *'cried Wolf?'*" complained Python.

"Don't change the subject!" snorted Mole.

And then the wind returned. A short, cold gust popped the limp sails open and jerked the vessel forward. Then, after a foreboding pause, the tempest hit full force. With her sails full, the schooner buried her rail and plunged through the rapidly-growing seas.

"Help!" cried Captain Wolf over the roaring wind. "With the compass not working, I'm not sure where to steer us but even if I did, I'm fighting this wheel. I can't control the ship!"

A great gust heeled the schooner over. Spray flew. Waves crashed over the deck and the three travelers clung to the cabin top, praying that their vessel wouldn't roll over. With a groan and a whoosh, the foresail exploded into tatters.

"Look!" called Python. "She's standing up!"

"She's back under control," shouted Wolf!

"There must have been too much sail up!" cried Mole. "Let's get this big one down!"

Python and Mole wrestled the mainsail down and lashed it to the boom, and due to some clever intercut scenes of lines moving through blocks and the sail descending the mast, the story never had to reveal how Python could have been of any use whatsoever.

"She's steering more easily now … but where do I steer to?" asked Captain Wolf. "What's our heading?"

"That compass is about twenty degrees off based on how we had to adjust our course to round the marker in chapter 6," said Python. "Just steer that much off-course and we should end up more or less *on*-course!"

"I suppose there's nothing more we can do," said Captain Wolf. "But though the wind is stronger than I'd like, the storm has changed its direction. Instead of blowing in our face, it's blowing from behind us. If our course is true, we'll make port in half the time."

"That's good," said Mole. "I'm feeling a bit queasy."

"Skip it," advised Python. "Storybook characters don't puke, either."

"I'll stay at the wheel," suggested Captain Wolf. "You boys go below and get dry and warm. Plus, that will give you a quiet and comfortable place to wrap up this chapter without the added complexity of a third character's voice."

"Good thinking," said Python. "Thank you, Captain!"

Mole shook out his fur and followed the incapable-of-getting-wet Python down the companionway hatch into *Clementine's* cabin.

"I've got some ideas to run by you," said Mole to Python once they were comfortably seated. "I think I've figured out a few things about stories."

"Tell me,"said Python.

"Well, the difference between an anecdote and a story is that the story has some sort of lesson buried in it. The anecdote version of what happened is that a blast of wind blew out the foresail. That's just a recounting of a factual event—journalism…"

Python nodded.

"…but the *story* version of what happened is metaphorical. With too much sail up for the high winds, the boat heeled over and became difficult to control. That's a lesson our readers can apply to life and business."

"I think I understand," said Python.

"Some people might think that more sail equals more progress," continued Mole, "but a sailboat can only go so fast. Once she hits her maximum speed, she heels over more and puts her rail underwater, the sails and rigging get strained, and you end up dragging the rudder sideways through the water to keep her on her course."

"That must be it!" agreed Python. "That's why Captain Wolf couldn't steer the boat. *Clementine* was overpowered."

"Yes," agreed Mole, "and the foresail blew out to teach us that important lesson. How often do we see a business—or a child or a romance—try to grow too fast? It's counterintuitive but sometimes the best way to stay at maximum speed and maneuverability is to take *down* some canvas. You'll go just as fast with less sail up and you'll enjoy a much more comfortable ride. That's not journalism; that's *journey-ism*."

"Excellent," said Python. "And I sense that the personal value story you've been struggling to tell is also beginning to emerge."

"What do you mean?" asked Mole.

"Sorry but that's part of this chapter's cliff-hanger," replied Python. "I'm supposed to say that and leave our readers hanging so they'll come back to us in chapter 8."

"That's okay," said Mole. "I'm excited about these new story insights. I can wait to let my own story unfold. How many chapters do we have left to go anyway? Can't be many."

"It feels like the seas are calming some," observed Python.

"Yes. I'll brew some tea for us. I'm sure Captain Wolf will appreciate a hot mug."

"But it's too early for the chapter ending," said Python. "We've only been down here talking for a few minutes."

"I've got it!" exclaimed Mole. "We're cold and exhausted. How about we fall asleep for a few hours and *then* make the coffee?"

"It was tea," said Python, "but yes, an excellent idea. Cue the narrator."

Cold and exhausted, Mole and Python wrapped themselves in blankets and lay on the soft, comfortable cushions in *Clementine's* warm cabin. Soon they drifted off into that deep and restorative slumber that only the sailor knows. The hands on the ship's clock spun rapidly to indicate the passing of the hours.

"Hey Mole," said Python. "You awake?"

"I am now," said Mole. "Thanks."

"I guess that is one of the world's stupidest questions," said Python. "Sorry."

"I'll get that coffee going," suggested Mole.

"Tea," corrected Python. "Storybook characters usually drink tea."

"Gotcha."

Mole carried three warm mugs of tea up to the deck of the schooner. The skies had cleared and the wind had abated, though it continued to blow from a favorable direction. Captain Wolf had raised the big mainsail again and *Clementine* skimmed playfully over the waves.

"Thanks for the tea, gentlemen," said Captain Wolf. "I do have some coffee down in the galley if you … well … never mind." She extended a paw toward the bow of the boat. "Keep your eyes forward. Whenever we get to the top of a big wave, you can make out the lights of the harbor on the horizon. We've made record time!"

"How about you let me steer for a bit," suggested Mole. "It's easy enough to aim for the harbor lights. Go get some rest, Captain Wolf. I'll wake you when we get close to the harbor."

The moon set and the clouds cleared, revealing the Milky Way's infinite ribbon of stars. Python and Mole watched in silence as the lights of Port Metaphor grew closer and closer.

8

StorySailing®

A T FIRST LIGHT, as soon as the schooner
Clementine was moored to the pier at
the base of Mount Metaphor, Captain Wolf de-
parted with a wink and a wave and scampered
down the dock.

"I wonder what's got her in such a hurry,"
mused Mole. "We're a day early. You'd think
she'd want to…"

"There's no telling," replied Python. "Maybe
she's adding a note of mystery to the plot."

"Ah … narrative tension. It never hurts a story, does it?" noted Mole.

The two travelers bid the schooner *adieu* and proceeded up the dock to the shore. "This will be our final ascent," said Python, "our last slope to climb before we meet Fox."

"How exciting," exclaimed Mole. "I sure hope she can help me find my authentic value so I can communicate it to others."

"I suppose I should also help reinforce the plot and remind our readers why we're here," said Python. "We've come a long way. I'll be quite disappointed if Fox doesn't teach me any new hunting skills."

"Hey! There's even a story in that!" observed Mole. "Sometimes we make a choice to dedicate ourselves to a quest—a new direction, a new relationship, a new job, a new course of study—and right around chapter 8 we start wondering whether or not we made the right decision. Should we have stayed where we were? Kept our money? Taken the other fork in the road?"

"It's buyer's remorse," said Python, "and you're right. Those voices of self-doubt make a wonderful storytelling theme because they're the biggest obstacle we all face in life. The mountain presents a challenge on a *physical* level but the question of whether or not we will find the strength and determination to make the climb presents a *personal, spiritual* challenge. Why else would we climb it?"

"Because it's there...," said Mole, "but *it* isn't the mountain!"

Python nodded enthusiastically. "And I'm sure that's why this mountain is named..."

"Yes! Yes!" said Mole. "And this last segment of our journey—the sailing adventure—has got me thinking more deeply about stories and how they work."

"Well," said Python, "Carl Jung did say that water was an archetypal symbol for consciousness. It doesn't matter whether you're an Inuit or an Indian or an idiot. If you dream about water…"

"That's probably too heady for this book; it's supposed to sound like a children's tale," said Mole, "but I think the golden rule of storytelling is this:

STORIES ARE ALWAYS ABOUT PEOPLE!

"But Mole, we're talking animals!" said Python. "If stories are about…"

"Ah, but we are animals who engage in discussion and experience self-doubt," asserted Mole. "We *almost* get scammed by cheesy marketing pitches. We read road signs and hike and climb and sail. We set off on journeys in search of wisdom. *We are metaphorical people.* There's the mountain and there's the *mountain*. Stories are always about people!"

Python closed his eyes and took a few moments to ponder Mole's idea. "If you're right—and I suspect you are—that golden rule explains why so many advertisements and sales pitches and important lessons fail to make an impact. Billions of dollars are wasted every year because advertisers are talking about prices, processes, ingredients, and data. If you're not talking about people…"

"You're not telling stories!" said Mole.

"And if you're not telling stories, you're not connecting!" Python flicked his tongue.

"And if you're not connecting…" Mole extended a paw toward his friend.

"You're not selling!" exclaimed Python. "Good job! You've looped us back to chapter 1. If your goal is to influence *anyone* else to do *anything* else—even if that just means getting them to understand your perspective—you're selling."

"And that means we need to talk about meaningful human outcomes," continued Mole. "Our readers—*people*—don't care about square footage; they care about *living* space. They don't care about the five-step *process;* they care about how mastering a new skill or defeating an old habit will empower them to *survive.* They don't care whether the hiking stick is made of elm or oak or hickory; they care about how it will help ease their struggle up the mountain."

"You're onto something," encouraged Python. "So often, we don't address the *authentic* conflict. Deep down, we care about survival — about food, love, family, shelter, sex, status, safety. We don't care about the size or the process or the ingredients or even the price until we connect those things to a survival-level conflict."

The path wound up from the shore of the lake up through a lovely wood where red and gold leaves hung on the trees and carpeted the ground. Sunbeams filtered through the branches, and the twittering of birds and buzzing of insects encouraged the travelers on their way.

"That was a *delightful* narrative interruption," complained Mole.

"It had to be there," said Python. "While we're philosophizing, the reader needs to feel like something physical is happening. They need to know that our journey is continuing—that we're making progress on the path."

"I suppose," said Mole. "So where was I?"

"Actually, I had just finished talking about authentic, survival-level conflicts."

"Oh yes," said Mole. "And that—combined with our recent sailing adventure—suggests a simple way to explain how stories work. The *people* in our story—you and I and Captain Wolf—were stuck out on the rocky stormy seas of conflict. Our goal was to make it to the safe port of transformation."

"Good," said Python. "A story moves from conflict to transformation."

"But to make that passage safely, we need two more elements," continued Mole. "The first one is that the water has to be deep enough. We have to navigate around the marker or we'll run aground in the shallows. 'Deep enough' means the conflict has to be *authentic*."

"So," said Python, "when Captain Wolf told us we'd have to tack upwind and plot lines of the position on the chart…"

"All that jargon disconnected her message from anything we might find *meaningful*," said Mole. Because we didn't have a practical way to assess whether or not it made sense to sail aboard the *Clementine*…"

"We ended up making an emotional decision," said Python. "We *assumed* that Captain Wolf's technobabble meant she knew what she was doing — that we'd be in safe hands."

"And it turned out she knew no more about sailing than we did!" said Mole. "She just read her lines and…"

"I'll bet that happens all the time," said Python, "but doesn't that imply that technobabble is an effective hunting technique? It doesn't feel like what I've been looking for but it seems to have worked on us."

"It's *not* what you're looking for," said Mole, "because though you might keep your passengers paying while the wind is fair and the seas are calm, they'll jump ship after the first storm … assuming they survive. They'll see that you're just after their money — that you aren't in touch with their true, authentic conflict. It's only effective as a short-term strategy and even then…"

"Hey! Look at that rock!" exclaimed Python.

"I don't see anything special about it," said Mole.

"Sorry. I've been waiting for the writer to drop in another 'climbing-through-the-woodlands' narration to keep this chapter from getting too static."

"That wasn't a very good substitute," said Mole.

"He must be in the can," said Python. "That was the first thing that came to mind."

Mole cleared his throat. "So now that we're higher up the trail let's recap. We've covered conflict and transformation. And we decided that if the water isn't deep enough—if the conflict isn't an authentic one that we find *meaningful* because it affects us on a survival level, the boat—*the story*—won't be able to make the journey."

"And there's one more element that every sailing voyage needs," added Python.

"Wind!" exclaimed Mole. "Yes! Magic! A powerful, invisible force."

"Sounds a bit woo-woo to me," said Python.

"Not at all," said Mole. "Your wind—your 'magic'—can be your talent, a burst of insight, your experience, your creativity, your team—even your specialized equipment—anything that makes you unique—anything you can do or say that helps you blow *other people* toward *their* safe port of transformation!"

"Hmm," said Python. "Conflict, transformation, authenticity, and magic plus a golden rule. That's interesting, and it "suggests that what we're really doing here on our journey..."

"...is trying to find our magic," said Mole. "*That's* the mountain so many people are struggling to climb. They've been told they're not good enough or not smart enough or not pretty enough or not fast enough or that the path is just too steep for them. They can either give up and live a life without magic or they can keep climbing and hope to find it."

"I like it," said Python.

"And they hope," continued Mole, "that at the end of the climb—at the top of the mountain— they'll find some teacher, a wise Fox who will reveal the magic they've been struggling to find."

"Wow!" said Python. "I had no idea when I took this gig that we'd be playing such a leadership role. If we don't make it to the top and find what we're looking for…"

"Yep, our whole story will end up dashed on the rocks along with the hopes and dreams of our readers," said Mole.

Well at least that solves one problem that's been starting to weigh on me," confided Python.

"Me too," said Mole. "Now we have an authentic conflict to end chapter 8 with."

9

The Confidence to Climb

As Python and Mole climbed higher up the face of Mount Metaphor, the air began to thin and the brisk wind grew colder.

"This is tough going," complained Mole.

"Yes ... but that's to be expected," said Python. "We must be getting close to the end of the story. There's always a final struggle — a final challenge."

"I hope this is it," wheezed Mole. "I'm bushmeat!"

The two huffed and puffed their way up the steep slope, navigating around boulders and backtracking whenever the path dead-ended or led off a cliff.

The pair trudged onward and upward until Python paused and sniffed the air. "I think someone's following us," whispered Python to his friend.

"Way up here? I doubt it," replied Mole. "Why would you think that?"

"Rule of threes," said Python. "We met Jackal and then Captain Wolf. There almost certainly has to be one more."

"COME OUT!" called Mole. **"WE KNOW YOU'RE THERE!"**

"What are you doing?" asked Python, surprised.

"Getting on with it," said Mole. "How much bridge material do you want to read?"

On Mole's cue, a shabby creature crawled out from behind a rock. "Please don't eat me!" she cried.

Mole and Python looked at one another, pretending to be astonished just as the script directed.

"That's not going to happen," assured Python. "I'm vegan."

"And what do moles eat?" asked the timid third character.

"I have a few extra granola bars if you'd like one," said Mole. "Mostly we just line up at the food tent with the rest of the crew and see what they're serv…"

"Never mind that," interrupted Python. "Who are you and why are you following us?"

"I'm Coyote," said Coyote. "I heard you talking a long way back about going to see Fox. And since nobody has ever actually seen Fox, I thought I'd follow behind and find out what happens."

"Well that's great news!" said Python.

Mole shook his head. "I had no idea we might be hauling ourselves over this cold and unforgiving terrain for nothing! Are you sure? Everyone always talks about how wise and wonderful Fox is. If she turns out to be a myth…"

"Well *I* believe she's real," asserted Coyote.

"What have you heard, Coyote? What do you know?" asked Python.

Coyote stepped onto the path. "I've watched a lot of travelers drag themselves up this mountain … and I've watched them all go back empty-handed. I've also heard that Fox really is wise and generous, but you have to pass a test or answer a question or face some sort of challenge before you can see her."

"I should have guessed," said Python. "This is classic storytelling stuff. If you want to lift the curse, acquire the treasure, and marry the princess…"

"You have to slay the dragon!" said Mole, completing Python's thought.

"You have to prove yourself worthy," said Coyote.

"I'm tired. I'm running out of steam," complained Mole. "My paws hurt. Can you share any insights into how we might provide evidence of this worthiness?"

"I've watched a lot of people try," said Coyote. "Some offer blessings and sacrifices. Some have even tried to set traps so they can bring the mysterious Fox home as a prize. Others act very polite … for a while … until they get cold and hungry and tired of wandering around

Mount Metaphor pretending to be better than they really are."

"So you just stay up here watching?" asked Python.

"I'm only a lone coyote who lives up here on the mountain. I'm surely not worthy to be in the presence of the wise and wonderful Fox. I wouldn't know what to ask her if I did meet her and I have no gifts to give. But since I was a pup I've always wanted to…"

"You can climb with us, Coyote," offered Mole. "We'll either fail or we'll succeed but we've come this far. There's no reason for you to hide in the brush and sneak around."

"I agree," said Python. "Join us. If nothing else, you can help us crack jokes about the script."

Coyote's eyes grew large. "We can't do that! Surely the director will…"

"Never gonna happen," assured Python. "We get away with *murder* here. Think about it; where are they gonna find more talking animals? And besides that, we're almost at the end. They'd have to redo the whole production. I doubt they've got the budget for that."

The trio continued together, talking as they struggled up the trail.

"I do hope Fox is real," said Mole. "I hope we get to meet her and I could certainly use some wise counsel, but I'm not going to light any candles, rub any crystals, or sing any mantras. I'm just a humble mole seeking advice. I didn't schlep up this mountain to appease some diva."

"Shhh!" admonished Coyote. "Fox could be anywhere. She might hear you!"

"I'm with Mole," said Python. "I'll be respectful. I'll be grateful for any insights Fox might have to share, but it's not like she owes us anything. It's not like she *asked* us to haul our butts up this mountain."

"And you don't even have a butt!" quipped Mole.

"Is that really in the script?" asked the incredulous Coyote.

"Of course not!" said Mole, "but what can they do about it?"

"I thought this gig was gonna be a real snoozer," said Coyote.

"No, we have fun…," said Mole, "but there's a balance to it. You can fool around as long as you don't…"

"…get too far from the story," said Python. "So where were we?"

"You were talking about not getting too worshipful," said Mole to Python.

"Yes," explained Python. "Some people lead by asserting their authority and expecting everyone to bow and scrape and pay tribute. But if you were 'The Wise and Wonderful Fox'—resplendent with glorious alliteration and gilded capital letters—would you really want to hang out with a bunch of sycophantic pilgrims who all expect you to save them from certain idiocy?"

"That would be ample incentive for *any* sane person to take up residence on a remote mountain top!" agreed Mole.

Coyote looked down, deep in thought, "So the gifts you bring to Fox are...?"

"Stories from the road," said Python.

"Wisecracks about the script," suggested Mole.

"Comments about our odd experiences playing talking animals in a bizarre children's tale for businesspeople," added Mole.

"But I always thought I'd have to bring chocolates and an American Express platinum card!" said Coyote. "I have *nothing*. How could someone like me be worthy to see…"

"Worthy smurthy," interjected Python.

"Interesting how you have to spell 'smurthy' with a 'u' instead of an 'o,'" observed Mole.

"Otherwise it rhymes with 'more' and not with 'mirth,'" agreed Python.

"But back to you, Coyote," said Mole. "You're no different than anyone else. You doubt yourself and wonder if you're good enough … unless you're a raving narcissist. That's one of life's great challenges. *That's the mountain!*"

"Yes, and narcissism is the only disease in the world where the sicker you are the better you feel," added Python. "We meet too many people who feel *so good…*"

"And they're usually the ones who don't have much of a reason to," said Mole.

"Sometimes the biggest gift you can bring to someone worthy of giving it to," suggested Mole, "is a problem."

"How could that be?" asked Coyote.

"We all know people who come to us with a different problem every day. And no, that doesn't feel like much of a gift," explained Python.

"But when we're climbing up the trail," said Mole, "sometimes I ask Python to wrap his top half around a bush or a rock and send his tail down so I can shinny up."

"And I'm honored to be called upon to help," said Python. "Mole works hard to progress on the journey. If I can do something to help my friend succeed, it makes me feel good that he's gifted me the opportunity to do that."

"But I wonder, Python" asked Coyote, "Doesn't it get old? Seems like you're always the one doing the helping. Isn't balance important?"

"What *you* call 'balance' is really just 'keeping score,'" explained Python. "I will always be twelve feet long and Mole will always be one-twelfth that length. Why should I expect *him* to extend his tail and haul *me* up the trail?"

"But that sounds so unfair," protested Coyote.

"Not at all," said Python. "Except for that opening gag in chapter 1, I enjoy Mole's sense of humor. He shares thought-provoking insights and ideas. He's another pair of eyes and ears. Mole is my companion and my friend. I couldn't have made this journey without him; it would have been lonely and dull."

"Thank you, Python," said Mole. "You weren't cast in the previous chapter, Coyote, but the golden rule of storytelling is…"

STORIES ARE ALWAYS ABOUT PEOPLE!

"I love how you did that with the typography!" exclaimed Coyote.

"The point is," said Python, 'that the journey is more about the people we connect with than the ground we cover."

"The people we meet on the journey *are* the journey," added Mole.

"So stop beating yourself up," said Python to Coyote. "Cowering in the bushes and telling people you're worthless will never get you a seat at the table."

"Thank you," said Coyote with a tear in her eye.

The three journey-ists continued on, climbing higher and higher up the mountain above the clouds. Below them, they could see the terrain they'd covered—the shimmering surface of the great lake they'd sailed across and if they squinted, even the *wayyyy* distant wood where they'd started on their journey.

"Look!" said Mole. "It's another sign!"

"What is this?" exclaimed Python.

"There must be two more signs!" cried Mole. "Rule of threes. Keep climbing!"

A short distance down the path, the trio encountered another colorfully painted message:

Python grumbled. "I was expecting something a bit less..."

"Commercial?" asked Mole.

"Yes," said Python. "Perhaps a bit more elegant ... stately ..."

"Let's continue," suggested Coyote. "We're close! I can feel it."

Farther up the slope, another sign appeared.

"Almost there," called Mole. "We're almost there! *I know it!*"

And then there it was—a green wooden door with a rusty mailbox in front of it upon the side of which the name FOX had been scratched into the peeling paint.

"That's it?" exclaimed Python.

"I don't know what to say," said Mole. "It's just a door with a mailbox—not much different than my own."

"But I'm finally here!" cried Coyote. "I've always dreamed of this moment. If it weren't for you two friends, I would never have…"

"Go ahead," said Python.

"Yes," said Mole. "Go knock on the door."

"But you…" blubbered Coyote.

"We'll be right behind you," said Python. "We all got here. We all made the journey. Go have your moment. We can wait a little bit longer. Come get us when you're ready."

"I need to go find a bush anyway," said Mole.

"Thank you, Mole! Thank you, Python! I'm so…"

"Go," said Mole. "You're as worthy as anyone."

Coyote sniffed, then walked up to Fox's door and knocked.

She waited and knocked again.

Finally the door creaked open and Coyote slipped inside.

10

Journey's End

WHAT DO YOU SUPPOSE Fox has done to Coyote?" asked Mole.

"I'm worried, too," said Python, "It's been at least an hour since she went in."

"Should we…?"

"Yes," said Python. "Stay behind me."

The two travelers approached Fox's green door.

"Ready?" asked Python.

Mole nodded.

Python sprung at the door which offered no resistance. The pair tumbled through it.

"Hey, wait a second! This is the production lot! How'd we get here?" gasped Mole.

"The whole thing's a big set!" said Python.

"A big set-up!" sputtered Mole.

"Great!" said Python. "This is just great! How are we going to finish our story? If we leave readers hanging we'll never work again!"

"Let's walk over to the food tent and figure this out there," suggested Mole. "They've got Indian food today; the samosas are to die for."

Leaving Fox's front door ajar, they walked past a forest of lights and microphone stands and stepped over a carpet of cables to the tent around the corner from the set.

"Boy! Boys! I've been expecting you," called a silky voice. "The *saag paneer* is delightful.

Grab yourselves a plate and a cold drink. Come sit down."

Fox sat at a picnic table, her lovely red-brown bushy tail rising behind her.

"What have you done with Coyote?" demanded Mole.

Fox began to laugh. "Coyote…? I *am* Coyote!"

"I don't understand," said Python.

"Sit and I'll explain everything," said Fox. "Don't worry. We'll get our story finished! Go load up some plates and come sit. Get yourselves some curry and rice."

"Wait here," said Mole to Python. "I'll grab a plate for you. Doesn't look like there's any line at the counter."

"The crew still thinks you've busted into my den to confront me about Coyote!" Fox laughed again. "We have this place to ourselves until they get all the equipment moved and figure out we won't be producing that scene."

Mole carried two full plates over to the table where he rejoined Fox and the still-incredulous Python.

"What did you mean when you said 'I *am* Coyote?'" asked Mole.

"Oh that!" said Fox with a dismissive wave of her paw. "Coyote and Captain Wolf and Jackal— they were all me! I've been traveling with you from the beginning."

"Wow! Great disguises," said Mole. "I never had a clue."

"This place has an over-the-top costume department," explained Fox. "I could have come as Godzilla ... and you should see their Ironman suit! But in case you didn't notice, all the characters were canines. I wouldn't have made a very convincing octopus!"

"Buy why?" asked Python. "You've been playing us since day one!"

"Well darling, I am a fox! What did you expect?"

"I kinda hoped you were a different sort of fox," confessed Mole.

"Maybe I am and maybe I'm not," replied Fox. "But you did pass all my tests. You made it to the top of the mountain."

Python shook his head. "I'm not getting this."

Fox smiled slyly as foxes do. "If you had bought one of Jackal's silly branches, I'd have left you wandering up and down the trail buying all sorts of silly crap until you ran out of money and went home. I almost had you there, Mole, but Python saved the day."

"So it was *you* who laid down the mysterious footprints that led us to the dock?" asked Mole.

"Of course," said Fox. "And then I ran ahead, switched into my wolf costume, and waited aboard the schooner."

"But how did you learn to sail? How did you learn all that jargon?" asked Python.

"Let's just say I did a lot of sailing in a different life," said Fox. "But it was all in the script … and frankly, if you two had read it all the way through before we started, none of this would have been a surprise to you."

"Does anyone really do that?" asked Mole, raising an index claw.

"Hmm … probably not," replied Fox.

"They don't want to ruin the ending," suggested Python.

"I suppose most people just live their lives one page at a time," observed Mole.

"No, that's just how stories work," said Fox. "Nobody rides a helicopter to the top of the mountain; what would be the point? It's all about the climb—all about the struggle."

"So what was Coyote all about?" asked Mole.

"She was the final test," said Fox, "and it's not a test many people pass. You made it to the top of the mountain; you were all set to be the heroes of the story," explained Fox, "but the best storytellers are never the heroes of their stories; they're the ones who *guide others* to become the heroes."

Mole cut in. "So when we told Coyote to run ahead of us so she could experience her big dream moment…"

"Exactly," said Fox. "She didn't see herself as 'worthy,' but though you had your own struggles on the mountain, you decided to boost her confidence, help her discover her self-worth, and let her be the first to plant her flag on the summit. Good work!"

"Look Fox," said Mole. "I get it…. There's no guru on top of the mountain wearing robes and dispensing redemption and showering us with lotus blossoms. The real teachers are the regular folks we meet along the path. Some of them help us out and some of them get in our way and some of them get in *their own* way, but we can learn from all of them. But is that *all* there is to this story? Is *that* the lesson? Is that *it*?"

"There must be more to it than that," said Python. "What's the big payoff that makes the climb worthwhile?"

"I don't mean to be rude," said Mole, "but this Q & A is getting rather tedious. Could you just give us our Wizard-of-Oz moment?"

"Yes," agreed Python. "What happened to Mole discovering how to understand and communicate his authentic value? What about me learning some new prospecting techniques so I can keep up with the smart prospects?"

Fox licked her nose. "Okay Python, back in chapter 7 you mentioned you had some ideas about Mole's transformation. What were they?"

"Mole got taken in by Jackal's silly signs and blistery bluster," explained Python. "But after that, he started thinking deeply about stories and how they work. He came up with a golden rule and four elements. He discovered the difference between an anecdote and a story—between a journalist and a journey-ist. I'd say that Mole's *magic*—the invisible powerful force that distinguishes him from every other mole is his ability to *dig* deep into a story and mine the meaning."

"Good," said Fox.

"But that's easy," said Mole. "Digging is something I do naturally. What's so magical about that?"

"Mole, my dear," said Fox, "it's often the case that we have difficulty seeing our own magic. We take our talent for granted because anything we do with our super-powers will naturally be easy for us. Superman doesn't think, *Wow! Cool! I've got X-ray vision!* He just hopes Lois Lane doesn't bust him for staring at her and thinks his skills are no big deal; they're just what he does. But Mole, my friend Elephant would think your ability to dig tunnels is remarkable; he can rip a tree out of the ground but he can't tear up the links the way you do."

"I think Mole is a genius," said Python.

"And that's why it's so important that we connect with good and caring friends we can trust and depend on," continued Fox. "When we're with negative people who tell us what we *can't* do, we tend to believe them. When we surround ourselves with smart people whose judgment we trust and they tell us we're okay, at some point, we have to start believing them."

"But I'm no genius," protested Mole. "I just…"

"And it's best that you don't run around celebrating yourself as one," suggested Fox. "Geniushood is a title best bestowed by others and not by one's self… but do you trust Python's judgment?"

"I suppose," said Mole.

Fox smiled. "So you have a wonderful co-nundrum to ponder and leave your readers with. That's a good thing to end a chapter with and a good thing to end a story with. Having discovered that your physical digging skills are analogous to *metaphorical* digging skills, you now have to figure out how to use your magic to serve others. And even when you doubt your-self—which we all do, my dear—you have to consider that you have a trusted friend who says you're *worthy*."

"But how am I supposed to take this and…?" exclaimed Mole.

"Don't worry about that now," suggested Python. "That's a different story."

"Thank you, Fox," said Mole. "I have a lot to think about … but Fox, what about Python? What about new prospecting techniques? What was Python supposed to learn from Jackal and Captain Wolf and Coyote … and you?"

Fox shook her head and began to laugh. "Give me a moment," she sputtered. "I've been waiting to spring this on you since page 1!"

"Wait," said Python. "Did you…? Are *you* the one who wrote this…?"

"Yes and no," said Fox. And with that she reached her paws behind her head, fumbled around with the latch, and removed her head. Extending from the body of Fox's fox costume grinned the face of a man.

"Now *this* is getting weird!" said Python.

Mole gaped mutely.

"I'm Dave," said the man in the fox costume. "I wrote the script you two have been griping about since we started this story. My name's on the front of it in case you didn't notice!"

"Okay … but what does that have to do with prospecting?" asked Python.

"Everything," said Dave. "Anyone who's come this far is almost 15,000 words into the world's longest long-form sales letter! It's a commercial!"

"A commercial?" gasped Python, "But…"

"If this isn't an effective plug for the power of storytelling, I don't know what is!" said Dave. "And that's it! Storytelling is your prospecting technique … and anyone who's read this far has pretty compelling proof that it works!"

"But don't you think our readers will feel like you tricked them?" asked Mole.

"Some may," explained Dave, "but I'm not really a fox and those aren't really my intentions. Think about it: I didn't hammer a cheesy sign into anyone's trail and implore them to buy anything from me. I took them on a journey and I offered them useful ideas. Hopefully I made them laugh and think. And though some people will walk away, none of them can say I didn't invest in the relationship."

"Are you getting this, Python?" asked Mole.

"I think so," replied Python. "On a certain level it's just basic manners. Hunting—prospecting—selling—is just a process of offering value before you ask for anything. Like you'd do in any relationship you care about, you have to *demonstrate* that you're *worthy*. And to do that, you need to inspire people to believe it makes sense to pay attention."

"Which is what storytelling does," said Mole. "Bloviating about prices, processes, ingredients, and data won't work. Tell stories about how people can use *your* magic to move from *their* authentic conflict to a meaningful transformation…"

"And they'll see you as a guide and *ask* you for the business," said Dave.

"It makes sense," exclaimed Mole.

"So Python, you're good?" asked Dave.

"Yes," said Python. "I'm still a little shocked … but I too have plenty to think about."

"I have one more question if I may," said Mole.

Dave smiled. "Of course."

"What's in this for you, Dave? Are you hoping to sell books? I don't get it."

Dave took a sip of his tea before answering. "Selling books would be fine. If people enjoy our story and it makes them think and laugh, our story will be a success. But I'm not selling a story; I'm selling *storytelling*. All over the world people are struggling to tell stories that connect and engage. Bad storytelling costs billions of dollars and it generates a heap of sorrow. A CEO tells a story the wrong way and shareholder value tanks. A politician tells a story the wrong way and people start fighting in the streets. An entrepreneur tells a story the wrong way and an important, save-the-world idea doesn't get funded."

"Nice rule of threes there!" observed Python.

"Thanks, Python," said Dave.

"So what's your strategy?" asked Python.

"It's simple but readers can find out more about me in the back of the book. This story is about *you* and your journey to the top of the mountain to discover the power of storytelling. You're the heroes; I'm just the guide."

"Come on!" said Python. "Nobody ever reads the stuff in the back of the book! Once the story ends…"

"We'll just have to see," said Dave. "It's been a pleasure. Now go beat the lunch rush. Grab a few more samosas to take home. I won't tell."

About the Author

DAVE BRICKER spent years sailing in search of stories. Today, he's a speaker, presentation consultant, and business storytelling expert. If you want to say it, share it, or sell it, bring him your story; he'll help you tell it.

Discover Dave Bricker's StorySailing® keynote speeches, books, engaging professional development sessions, and "tough love" presentation coaching programs at storysailing.com.

Acknowledgments

I am blessed to enjoy the wise counsel and loving support of immensely talented friends.

My deepest gratitude goes to:

Will Ezell

Dr. Margarita Gurri

Caroline de Posada

Rosemary Ravinal

Zeynep A. Talu-Balci

Bruce Turkel

Books by Dave Bricker